Introduction

I can't help but admit that I am not very sure how to start this, or if it is even worth trying to write. I originally had the idea to write this and that it could potentially, one day even become a tool to help with the initial steps of therapy. For me, it is easier to write things out than it is to tell them all at once, and it is intended to be written from my perspective. This thought came to me while sitting outside of my apartment smoking a cigarette one day early in the year 2024. It was nowhere near the greatest time of my life, nowhere near to say the least. I was in between jobs, an arctic 3front had come down from Canada early that year that prevented me from getting to work. Losing my job, I was frantic, but I was thankfully able to get a new job rather quickly. It was only a matter of waiting for a few normal things to go through. Background checks, drug testing, the same things you have gone through while applying for a new job I'm sure. I wanted to speak out about my story, and that of my wife, to hopefully help some of those in need, or to even spread awareness about the harsh realities of mental health. I suppose that I should start from the beginning, but to tell you every detail of my life would be a very long, and somewhat windy boring story. To save us both the trauma, I will simply stick to the details that come to mind in the most linear manner possible. I hope that this helps anyone out there that is like me, and that you at the very least, can take something from this that will help or save someone in your life or future, past, present, any context that it may seem to fit. While reading through this you may notice certain grammatical errors, most of them are placed intentionally for you,

4the reader. If you should feel so inclined, you may correct my mistakes. Marking up your book, I left margins on the edges of the paper that should provide the space. Change my story, correct it in any way you see fit, where I could have added more detail, where something doesn't fit. Anything and everything you choose it's your book now!

Table Of Contents

Chapter Eight: Child Custody

Chapter Nine: Manipulation

Chapter Ten: More

Backstory

Growing up, I would not say that we were poor. At least, not to me, I was the youngest of 4 children. My mother and my father both had a child when they met. My mother had her son, and my father had a son as well. They met in a local bar in town one night, and the rest was history. Having my sister and me, another son a few years later in life. We unfortunately had to experience death early on in our life, losing three out of four of our grandparents before I was ten years old. My grandmother and grandfather, on my father's side, and my grandmother on my mother's side. Given that we lost our grandparents early on, we did not live a bad life by any means. We had access to everything and then some that was needed for a stable environment to live in. We were not excessively poor, or excessively wealthy, if anything I would say upper of the lower class. That is until later in life where we became middle class, which I will explain shortly. My brothers, being several years older than myself or my sister, were unfortunately required to take on more responsibilities at a younger age. The normal things that are expected of older siblings. To help with the chores around the house and watching after my sister and me. All the normal qualities of life we had during our upbringing; we were loved. Very much so, celebrating every holiday and having family gatherings with extended family. Looking back and reminiscing now as an adult, we had a very good life. Which brings me to myself, and why my childhood took a dark twist in my mind. You see, my brothers were much older than I was. My father was a very rough, tough man who believed in disciplining his children. Instilling good manners and discipline was very important to him. He never "beat" us, so to speak, and never laid a hand on my sister Megan. Because he did not believe in disciplining his girl physically. Us boys, however, was a different story. As a parent now, I may not go to the same lengths that he did, given the times, it was much more socially accepted in the nineties to discipline your children than it is now in the 2020s. While my brothers were growing up, they were subject to a younger, more hot-headed version of my dad, which gave them some distinct advantages in life, though they may not have viewed it in the same ways that I did. They were always better at sports, and cooler, more well-rounded than I was. Able to fit in anywhere they went, they were both great at football, and sports in general, playing all throughout high school, getting scholarships either through academics or sports. Our dad was able to coach sports for us growing up, keeping us all in football or baseball, soccer, anything to keep us active. While I do enjoy outdoor activities, I got my first taste of video games in 1997, at four years old. It was relatively new technology at the time, Donkey Kong on the Nintendo 63. Then not much alter, Doom on the original PC. I fell in love with video games at a very young age, and science, just learning in general. I loved to read and explore my imagination. Fantasy worlds were incredibly intriguing to me, both today and as a youth. And at some point, I must have lost sight of that. It made me feel inferior to my brothers who were jocks in a sense, and though I did not know it at the time. I know now that I was depressed that I wasn't more like them. It took me a long time, and years of reflection, and unfortunate circumstances to understand my childhood better. Why would I even care to understand my childhood, you may ask? For now, I will say that in Elementary

School, I remember feeling on top of the world, like nothing could touch me. I had friends, people liked me, up until about the third grade. Where I felt like I was being made fun of for enjoying learning. My situation at school mimicked my home life. Not that I was made fun of at home for being a nerd. I was just different than my brothers or sister growing up. In middle school, I became very unhealthy, gaining an excessive amount of weight at a very early age. I was bullied in school for it, to the point that I became the guy that was always tugging at his shirt, tucking his stomach into his pants. I had stretch marks all on my legs, and stomach from gaining so much weight. It was embarrassing to be outside without a shirt on. My self-esteem was very low. In short, I began to hate myself early on, even though it may not have looked like it at the time. I was just a kid that did not understand what was wrong with me. I was active, perhaps not active enough, but I did go outside, and was very active. Perhaps not active enough, I don't really know why I gained so much weight, perhaps puberty. Or stress from being depressed, but I do remember that it angered my dad. Not so much that I was out of shape, but that I was unhappy, and he didn't know what to do to counteract that. Until one day, when he was doing better financially, working as a Postmaster for the Post Office, finally collecting his VA benefits from the military. He made some new friends that were into racing cars, so he bought a racecar. It was a 1969 Chevrolet Vega, a beautiful car, and we all started going racing together. My dad was obviously the one driving the car. I felt cool again, like I was a part of something. I was never very good at fitting in with sports, or anything for that matter. But racing cars with my dad? That was badass, one of those fantasy worlds coming to life, in my own life. My dad unfortunately had diabetes and was not the greatest at taking care of himself. When I was fourteen years old, he passed away from massive heart failure. He was only forty-six years old. It was devastating to myself and my family. But no one knew how to process the loss, because of the nature of my dad, he was a hard man. So, it was hard to mourn his loss, because it was not something that he would have wanted. He was a bit of an asshole at times, I will not lie, but he was a great man. Working hard for his family and making sure that we were all taken care of. Doing his best to try to provide and have fun at the same time with his wife and kids. Always buying our mother gifts on every holiday, taking her out when he could, teaching us the right way to be a man. He would have wanted us to be happy, and not mourn him for an extended period. Celebrate his life, not dwell in sadness about him moving on to a better place. As an adult, I truly idolize my father, and hope that everyone in the world has a moment to reflect on their father. Good, bad or terrible, and appreciate all the small things that they constantly did for their family. Even if they left, they may have in their hearts known that it was best for their child. Even if they gave you a bad example, which my father did on numerous, countless occasions. That's okay, because he was teaching us what not to do. In a time when he was doing that he had to do, being who he had to be, in a world that will take you out at the knees if you let it. After his passing, my life took a very weird turn. He left us a large sum of money when he passed, another thing that he did for us to always remember him. So, at the time of grief, we had joy. Because we had never known money before like that, my mom bought a new house. We had all worked together in our old house, putting in hundreds of hours of work to remodel the insides and out as a family. At the time I remember being quite upset about my mom wanting to get a new house. I wanted to remember my father and for the life of me, I couldn't understand why she wouldn't. Now that I am older, I can't imagine the pain that it would have caused her every day. Everywhere you look being a constant reminder of the pain from what we lost. There were memories written in every nook and cranny of that house. In Highschool, I was never very good at fitting in either, I can't say that I ever was prior either. And I don't really believe that Elementary School counts. There are probably those that don't believe it, but in my mind, I was not a part of any group in school. I was just me, a guy who lost his dad and shut himself off from the world. Until I met a girl, who helped me break out of my shell. I remember never feeling happier, I felt like I had the answer. Knowing what I wanted to do, I got a job at seventeen. Hoping to move out and get our own place together, figuring out life. To start building a future, I was beyond excited for the future and possibilities that it held. Shortly after Highschool, when she decided to go to college, she split up with me. Devastating my world. The old cliche I guess you could say, sad but true. Again, at the time, I was pretty upset about it. It caused me a whirlwind of emotions, I didn't know at the time, but she had become my way of coping with the stress of losing my father. Losing her, I felt like I was losing my dad all over again. Beyond just losing her, it was what she did to me that really took my mind on a whirlwind. We were together for quite some time, years, and she cheated on me, which I forgave, only to wind up telling me that if I was different, it would have been different. Maybe she wanted to be free, to have fun and not feel tied down. To this day I've still never been told the truth, only that if I was different, then it could have been different. I never viewed myself as a controller, maybe I wasn't fun enough. I'm not sure. But it left me devastated, questioning everything because she always seemed happy. She was her own person and was allowed to make whatever choice she wanted to. A few years after we split, after three or four years wasted at this point, we decided to try again. Big mistake on my part, I know, it was just a few days. Only for me to be told the same thing again. That if I were different, then it could have been different. Because I couldn't stop trying to prove to her that I was different, I turned to drugs and alcohol, among other things to tone her out of my mind. I didn't understand at the time that in my mind she was the only way for me to not have to face the death of my father. It was a rough lifestyle, working in bars, doing pills, cocaine, drugs in general, drinking every night, still a loner. Just me working and doing my own thing, no real purpose in life besides drugs and alcohol. It is amazing what depression can do to your mind, and what simple words can turn you into. She really did a number on me, sleeping around with everyone that I knew. And I don't say that to be mean, she really did sleep with most of the people that I knew, simply a fact. You may ask how or why it matters or affected me, but I always defended her. And never believed when people told me what she was doing. Passing it off as gossip or rumor. Which sucks for me, because the image I had of her in my mind was of someone that could never do that me. But as I said before, she was allowed to do whatever it was she wanted to do. We do live in a free world after all. In high school I had a close-knit group of friends.

Myself and three others, I won't go into detail about any of our many escapades. That would not only take a year and a half to get through them all, but most of the memories have turned into something sour. I will say that we had our share of fun. I unfortunately didn't find out for years, that she was also having sex with one of my good friends. Not to mention a lot of other people around the school and town. It made me look like a fool for defending her, or just a nice guy, either way, I felt like a fool. But she did some evil stuff I will say, now looking back at it at thirty years old. Granted we were in high school, and young, I don't believe that it justifies any of what she did to me. Some say that to have loved and lost is better than to have never loved at all. But I say to them that they have never loved someone and been cheated on and made to look like a fool. It is genuinely one of the worst feelings in the world.

Especially when you have defended that person for years, building them up. This may all sound like sadness so far, but there were a lot of good moments and happiness in my early life. However, most of them are not stories that I would feel comfortable writing down in a book. So, I will say that I am simply documenting the points that lead to me having an unfortunate meeting with my other self.

Meeting My Wife

At the age of twenty-three I joined the United States Army, as an Unmanned Aerial Systems Repairer. Working on long range drones, I found myself again. Boot camp, and AIT were both not very much fun, but the comradery you find with other people that are very similar to you makes it much easier to get through. I like many others made it through and on to my unit, it was a pretty good time, combined with very toxic shit. It's hard to say if I really did enjoy it or if we were all so traumatized by all the toxicity, we were just dealing with it and that amplified the fun we could have. I'm not entirely sure. But I will say that I don't regret any of it. Because of it, I was able to meet my wife. She is, and was an amazing woman, and mother, even more beautiful than Cleopatra herself in my eyes. She loves to sing; I fell in love with her the night I met her. In part because she was fearless, and beautiful and was up there singing karaoke in front of a whole bar full of people meanwhile making them drinks, and just being the life of the bar. She was literally everything that I wasn't, it's hard to explain it. Which makes it so much harder to write this and tell my story, the last thing that I want is for her to feel like anything about me is her fault, or her presence in my life could have caused any of my turmoil. I met her when I was out with some friends. She was the bartender, and I thought she was beautiful and naturally tried to talk to her. We hit it off pretty good from the bat, and before we knew it, we were dating. She told me early on that she had a daughter and a pretty messed up relationship with her ex. About a month into dating, she opened to me further about the extent of that relationship. She met her ex, and things seemed great, until she got pregnant and didn't want to be as sexual anymore. Normal things that happen to a woman during pregnancies, I for one cannot imagine the whirlwind of emotions that they have to deal with. Regardless of that, he was not happy with not receiving sexual favors, or the situation that he was in, wife pregnant and he was frustrated, whatever the case was. Thats when the cheating and beating began. He started putting his hands on her, beating her up, cheating on her, leaving her bloody and bruised. When she finally worked up the courage to leave him, he manipulated her into feeling bad for him. As most narcissists would do, I'm sure everyone has met one, perhaps even one as extreme as this guy. He made her believe that they would work together for 50-50 split custody and what's best for their daughter. All she had to do was hand over custody of their daughter to him, pending her getting back on her feet and not try for alimony or child support. She should never have fallen for it, but she did, and trusted him to keep his end of the deal. When we met all of this was already in motion, but I decided when she told me that I wanted to be a part of her life. And I didn't want to allow this to happen to her. He was hell bent on making sure that she would never see her daughter again, leaving the state of TN with her and refusing Keiarra any information on where she was or what he was doing. Having been a stay-at-home mom, not working and no savings, she didn't have the means to bring it to court, or have her voice be heard. So, she was powerless in the beginning to do anything to change the situation. From what I have seen, she is an amazing mother, and woman, and wife. I can't for the life of me understand why he wouldn't want her to be a part of her daughter's life honestly. It bewilders me. But then I remember everything he did to her and it kind of makes sense. Every day that he looks at their daughter is a constant reminder of what he did to her mother, but he believes that her mother did him wrong claiming that she was the one being unfaithful. He attempted to try to slander her reputation to me when we met, telling me she was a cheater and gave him an STD. To this day I have never had an STD or believed that she has ever cheated on me. Given my experience with girls, I do not take that lightly. So, I will not lie, I was somewhat unsure in the beginning of our relationship, I was in love with her, but her past relationship was complicated, so I did tread lightly in the beginning until I got to know who he was. Anyways, he was cheating on her and beating her up. But the story is always flipped, and it will go back and forth and not get anywhere because he will never tell the truth and claim that everything that she says is a lie. He is one of the most toxic people that I have ever met in my life, quite honestly. Shortly after their divorce, she got a house, job, car, everything that she needed to be considered back on her feet enough to have her daughter. And he still refused to work with her. Even going as far as to have it put in paperwork that she wasn't allowed to have over the night guests of the opposite sex, trying to maintain that control that he felt he had over her. He told her he would use every low blow he could, saying anything he had to in court to prevent her from having her daughter, even going as far as to say she was an alcoholic because she had a bottle of wine on her birthday and put it on social media. Meanwhile, he has photos on his social media of him and his military friends drinking straight from bottles of tequila. Mind you a bottle of wine shortly after having her daughter taken away from her, being forced out of her home, and having to go through court meanwhile trying to get her life back on track while fighting to keep her daughter in her life. Simply having a bottle of wine, after all that, does not quantify an alcoholic in my book, just a normal human if you ask me. He was playing hide the baby at the time, not allowing my wife any information on where she was, passing her back and forth between his family members because he didn't have the means to care for her on his own. To then finally meet a girl who eerily resembles my wife and marry her. Because at this time she was fed up, and taking him to court for more time, he didn't have any way to prove that he could care for the child without requiring assistance of family or another woman. Having to work, it wouldn't make sense for a small child to be forced to go to daycare. Despite all of this, being the wonderful person that she is, she still only wanted 50-50 split custody with him. Sharing the small child instead of fighting over her, trying to force the other parent out of her life. Keeping it fair and even, she was able to fight for 50-50 and got it for a short time. Until he decided to put their daughter into preschool and say that my wife is to have her only on the weekends because she is starting school. The courts, and my wife being powerless to stop this, had no choice but to comply. It was around this time that my wife and I lost our sons twin during childbirth as well. She developed pre-eclampsia and advanced help syndrome that led to losing one of our children. To this day I still believe that the stress of him, what he did to her, leading her on, fighting for her daughter, playing with her mind, etc. Put an extreme and excessive amount of stress on my wife that was the direct leading cause to the loss of our child. I have never hated anyone before, but I can honestly say that I hate this guy, and everything about him for it, still to this day. Seeing firsthand the result of the abuse and treatment of my wife, and now their daughter. Being powerless to stop it because the courts believe that they cannot intervene unless there is a threat to the health of the child. It doesn't say anything about mental health, simply their health, are they alive and have the means to live. Allowing him to do this for so long has powered his mind in a sick and twisted way. Give a narcissist a taste of power and they will never give it up. Fast forward and their daughter is now seven years old. We decided that we are going to move to Georgia to be closer to her because they have shown no intentions of having a better relationship with us. Regardless of them constantly telling us that they want to be friends with us. When we told him that we are planning to move to Georgia to be nearer to her so that both of our families can enjoy time with her, and she can have a chance to be a part of a much larger family. Now, this entire time his new wife, believes that he wants to have a better relationship with us, and doesn't understand the full implications of what he is doing. And if she does, then they are both exhibiting signs of extreme psychotic behavior. We simply cannot come to understand what they believe they are going to accomplish by trying to cut us out of their shared daughters' life. Believing that we are terrible people, or drug addicts, alcoholics, which couldn't be further from the truth. I will not lie we have indulged in alcohol, and marijuana, but that alone does not make anyone an unfit parent or person in anyway. We have been in and out of court for six years now, and just can't do it anymore. It's a crazy case, and it would take a lot of money and time to have a full trial for it, she has kept proof of all his abuse. The way that he talks to us, tries to manipulate and keep control, beating their daughter for "lying" about what he deems the truth. The psychological torment that he is putting everyone through simply because he refuses to acknowledge that it is him that does not want a healthy relationship, is enough to make you want to pull your hair out. Being powerless to stop it because you must have money to take them to court every single time. It's all crazy nonsense, and she never wanted to ruin his life or cause him any stress by telling the truth about it all. But at this point, I don't care anymore. It's time that it is heard what he has done to her and her daughter. Because it affects millions of people everywhere, we have said for years that the way that he is manipulating the courts should be taken all the way up to supreme court. I can't imagine how many people out there are under the torment of someone just like him, and it's enough to make you go crazy. It's the reason that people snap and do crazy stuff to the people around them. Because someone somewhere is treating them like they are crazy, spinning everything they say, making them doubt themselves and everyone around them. No one should be allowed to do what he has done. It's disgusting behavior, bringing false evidence and trying to attack and falsely damage the figure of the other person, defamation, slander all kinds of things. But to get it to stop you must spend thousands of dollars on lawyers and prove it all. It doesn't make sense why the courts have been set up the way that they are, almost a popularity contest, or who can throw more money around instead of obviously what's right and wrong. It seems that it is all about who do you believe in more or trying to just keep a middle ground. Anyways, after all this, he still doesn't want to have a good relationship, we asked for 50-50 again if we move within twenty miles of their home in Georgia. To which they say they can't guarantee more time, which is laughable because they are the only ones preventing more time in the first place. Granted we understand she is in school and living in separate states makes having more time during the week practically impossible, we are trying to resolve the issue forever, by relocating closer to them. At which point they just make up more excuses and reasons as to why we can't have more time. He has told us that we don't have a house, that I have built nothing for myself, all kinds of shit that is really messed up. If there is anyone that I have ever met that meets the true definition of a bully, and a senseless bully at that, it's my wife's ex-husband. He tried to claim that I was a pedophile, because I met and married a woman that has a child. Which is laughable, because what was my wife supposed to do, become a nun because she had his baby? Saying that had never built anything for ourselves, that were bad parents, we don't do what's best for our children, he has said an extreme number of terrible things to my wife and I that have led to extreme feelings of self-doubt, because he says them at times when we are in fact not in the best place. My wife and I believe that life has its ups and its downs, and you always must take the good from it no matter what, not put other people down when you're doing good, and they aren't. Life can always flip around, and that same person be doing better than you at a different time.

DON'T DO IT

I tried to kill myself in October of 2023. Don't worry I'll tell you the reason, but it's not going to be quite what you think. I have never been suicidal, even on that day, all throughout my life, ups and downs, kicked around, what have you. I have never once thought I'd be better off dead. Even the night that I tried to kill myself, that's not what was going through my head. It's very hard to talk about, and makes my stomach turn just thinking about it. But I took a box cutter and jammed it in my throat one night. I have been struggling with mental health since I got out of the military and we lost our daughter during childbirth, not to mention all the other death and stuff that has happened in my life. Losing my dad, grandparents, friends, girlfriend, then to lose Keiarra and I's daughter, not having a job, scraping by, there was a lot of reasons to feel like it would be better to end it. And I never once had that thought. Let me back up a little bit in time before I get too far ahead of myself. My first brush with my mental health problems was in 2021 at 27 years old. My wife and I moved back to my home in Florida after losing a child during childbirth in 2020. It was here that I was working, trying to provide and get us back on our feet, meanwhile fighting for my wife's daughter, and just trying to hold it all together. It took its toll. And I had a mental breakdown, no one knew what to do, because it was extreme. It wasn't me, and I don't know how to explain that, but it was literally like someone else was behind the wheel, and I was watching through a mirror like in a horror show. I didn't do anything too crazy when it happened, just a lot of yelling and rambling on about God and space and the universe. The ambulance came, I was taken to the hospital, where I eventually went to a place called life streams, a behavioral health facility. I don't have much memory of all of this, I am going based off what was told to me, and what I have read in the reports. I apparently had another mental breakdown while being admitted to the facility, where I broke out of the facility, and stole one of their vans, driving off running away from the police. They said that I got a few miles away and the tire popped, where I stopped and got out near a neighborhood. Where they say I tried to steal a vehicle from a woman, she punched me in the face and I ran away, thankfully, even being out of my mind I didn't hurt her or anyone in any of this. Then when the police caught up with me, I was taken to jail, on charges of grand theft auto, and carjacking without a weapon. There was no mention of the life streams visit, or that having an impact on my being arrested. Jail was not a pleasant experience, I was put on a massive number of drugs, more than anyone should be given in my personal opinion. I was stripped naked and put in a smock and slept on a cot for 3 weeks, given what they call beef patty and chips to eat. I essentially starved and hallucinated in another world for 3 weeks rotting in a cell. Being paraded around like an animal, tazed and treated like a crazy person. At one point it was stated that I crawled to the cell door after psychotherapy and was taking my medicine well. After 3 weeks of torture, I was taken back to Livestreams and dropped off. Where it took me several weeks to rehabilitate back into the real world. Coming out of the trauma of what they put me through while I was in jail, and from the mental breakdown that initially caused the spiral to happen. I know that three weeks

41

does not sound like a very long time, but it was a lifetime to me, and I can't imagine what those who have been through it for longer are going through personally. It is not a fate that I would wish upon my worst enemy. What they did to me while I was in there was horrendous, and it wasn't even the inmates. It was the guards, and the workers themselves. I don't know if it was hallucinations or if it was all real, but it was terrible. I don't remember much, but what I do remember was not something that I would want for anyone. I'm still, and forever will be probably recovering from it. I was tazed 6 different times, until I defecated all over myself and the room. I apparently tried to hang myself with my smock, from my bed frame. It was not a great experience, and like I have said, I do not remember but bits and pieces, but what I do remember, is truly horrific. Maybe it was a trauma response that shut off my mind so that I can't remember what was being done to me, or my mind was under so much stress that something happened inside it to distort the memories. Anyways, I began seeing therapists and psychologists immediately after I was released from life streams. They say that my mind did indeed split from extreme stress. But are unsure of what to label my condition as, whether it be multiple personality disorder, bipolar, ADHD, they are not sure. I started working again, taking a decent job all things considered as a maintenance technician for an apartment community in Florida. After about eight months of daily medicine, I was feeling back to normal, as normal as possible with everything that had happened to me in a short time. I wound up losing my job about 7 months later, 13 months after I got out of jail. My wife and I decided to move to TN, taking my wife's mother's offer of staying with her for some time to save money prior to getting our own place. After about one month we were unable to continue staying with her, due to unforeseeable circumstances that arose. We decided to secure an extended stay community for a few months until we were able to get into an apartment, which wound up taking about a month. Once we got into our apartment, we made the decision that we were for sure going to move to Georgia, to be closer to my wife's daughter. When we reached out to her ex-husband to inform him of our decision to move and whether they would still be interested in a 50-50 split custody arrangement, as they have stated multiple times that they want to work towards a better relationship. They responded with not being able to guarantee anymore time and that it would have to be up to a judge. Where they decided to file contempt paperwork against my wife for her moving to TN.

But why did you do it?

I still to this day don't know.
Apparently, my self does not like me very
much, or thinks I should do more regarding
my wife's ex-husband. I was having vivid
hallucinations of him murdering my wife's
daughter, my stepdaughter. Bringing her to
us because he refuses to accept that she
would rather live with us than him. Which
she has started multiple times at seven
years old. My mind was going over and
over again all the different things they could
say and do. It was pure mental torture, and
I don't understand why it happens. I sent a
bunch of text messages to them prior to it
happening. I do get slightly obsessed when
it comes to certain situations, this situation
with my wife and her ex being one of them.
Because I love my wife, I can't stand to

hear her daughter talk about being beaten by her father and not wanting to stay with her stepmother anymore. What they are doing to her is purely psychotic, brainwashing her into believing that her stepmother is her mother. Forcing her to call her mama or mom, which can have a dramatic effect on the mind of a child. And has had that effect on my stepdaughter. In a way I worry that I may be responsible for all this because I could have just turned the other way and not ever gotten involved. But then what kind of man would I be? What kind of husband would I be to my wife? This was all taking place in my mind at a hundred miles per hour. Repeating itself over and over again, and my mind is going over every possible detail trying to figure out some way to get them to understand why they should just work with us. That going to court and everything that comes with that is not healthy for my wife's daughter or for us, our small children or theirs. But they refuse to see any of that. I don't know if you have ever tried to change someone's mind before or get them to see things from a perspective that they refuse to try. But it is maddening. And in that madness of trying to reason with someone who is entirely unreasonable, my mind did something terrible. It almost made me a caveman, all sense and reason were out of the window, I truly felt like an animal this time. After about 4 days of not sleeping or eating, I was truly gone. And you can ask my wife, you wouldn't recognize me when it happened, I didn't recognize myself. But the fourth night, I apparently called my wife into our room, where I was bleeding out on our bed with a knife wound in my neck. Looking back and trying to remember that night is like being as drunk as you have ever been in your life, then doubling it, and taking a Xanax on top of it. I remember the feeling of an out of body experience, feeling like I was watching it all unfold with no power to stop it from happening. I couldn't put the knife down, I couldn't tell myself not to do it, I didn't have control of myself anymore. In short, I didn't try to commit suicide, My Self, tried to kill me. Which sounds crazy, but that's what it feels like in my mind. Because as I write this, watching my sons play in front of me, my youngest riding his toy car around the living room. My oldest with his boxing gloves on spinning in circles. My wife getting a few extra minutes of much needed sleep so that she can deal with two boys all day! I hate myself all over again for doing it to myself. Talking about it makes it better, and getting out your feelings helps. It's okay to feel vulnerable, and weak sometimes. The things people have said about me and to me my entire life combined with losing so much of my family growing up. It took a toll, and I should have opened up about how much of a toll instead of suppressing all of my feelings for such a long time. You never know who around you has been through something in their life, or is going through something or will go through something. No one is perfect, but we should all try to ensure that we are as kind as possible to everyone that we encounter. Whose path could be more windy or bumpy than our own path. They could have breaks in theirs, that they tell no one about. That you would never know about unless you caught them in the right or perhaps wrong moment.

Coping with it

It's not easy living after you've attempted suicide. Or your Self has tried to kill you, however you want to phrase it. There are days where I remember what I did and just want to bury my head in the sand for a few days. But I must move on, I have children, that need me here for them. I have a wife, that loves me, and cares about me, and would truly be sad if I ever left her. My sons would never forgive me for not being able to talk to them about life. To never be able to ask me why I did it. To never fully understand. I would never have been able to write this had my self been successful and the doctors weren't able to save my life. I get embarrassed when people try to talk to me about mental health, because I don't want anyone to know what I did. I have never really liked neck tattoos before, but I am contemplating getting one to cover up the scar on my neck now. I am thankful to God because I didn't leave any permanent damage that can't be healed, no damage to my throat, or breathing. It's a very weird experience to live through. So please, never do it, and if you do attempt it and live, tell yourself every day that it is okay. And then learn to re live, and keep on living, because the world is beautiful, and so is life if you give it a chance to show you. Even through so much death in my life, I still live believing that someday we will all be together again, and I can explain these mistakes that I have made in my life in a way that they will understand. Maybe I won't even have to explain it, I don't know, but i want to find out the right way. So that's how I cope with it, I just live every day, believing that everything I wish for in life will come true one day. There can't be good without bad, so to say that one day there will be peace on earth is a bit of a long shot, but we can all hope that that day will come. Maybe it takes something catastrophic, I sincerely hope not. But maybe it will happen, I make the conscience choice every day to not give up hope. To believe that my sons and stepdaughter can grow up in a world where good men, genuinely good people, get to win. To believe in a world where I get to meet everyone who I have lost, once again. My daughter, my father, uncle, cousins, grandparents. I have known death throughout my entire life, and I must make the conscious choice every day to know life instead. So should you. If you are, or even if you aren't going through some difficulties of your own in your life, take some time and answer these questions. Write your own short story, it has helped me to process everything that has happened in these recent years. Don't worry if you don't fill all the space at first, use it as a brainstorming tool to add more detail. Feel free to change the timeline as you see fit, if it was jail instead of high school or what have you, it's your story!

The Story of:

My childhood:

My time in Middle School:

My time in High School:

My life after I turned 18:

Why do I feel this way?

And how has it affected me on a personal level daily?

Reasons I choose to live:

Reasons I'd rather be dead:

What I look forward to in the future:

Why I feel empowered by my reflection:

My goals for the near and distant future:

In this section I will go into further detail about certain aspects of my life. The first section of the book is a brief short story that covers most sections of my life and then an exercise at the end to help cope with the immediate stressors in life. I hope that by going into further detail about certain things, it will help the readers to understand what is going through my mind at any given time of day. These things are not constantly on my mind, nor is negativity. However the weight everything that has happened to me, or I have done in my life do weigh heavily. Not only that, but there are those who have been through so much worse than me, that it makes me feel guilty for even feeling the way that I do at times. I can say it is hard to shake the way that it makes me. Perhaps together we can learn a way to healing, and our own truth.

Losing a child

I cannot begin to go into detail about the true pain that you feel when you lose a child. Our child was lost during childbirth, so there were not any memories of the child per say. So, I cannot comment on the pain of losing a child that is older or has impressed more on me than what I have already experienced. However, we had the anticipation of having twins. A boy and a girl at that. It was devastating that night that my wife woke me up, fear in her eyes. Trembling, she told me she wasn't feeling good, and I could see the pain she was in. Something was not right. So, we rushed to the hospital. It was there that I felt like I left a part of my soul behind. It was pure chaos from the moment we got to the hospital, where weirdly enough no one was at the receptions desk this night, so we went straight to the ER. Where they then told us that we needed to wait in the room to be called up, I tried to express to them that my wife was in excruciating pain, pregnant with twins, but also, she has preexisting conditions, and I was worried that she may be going into labor. They did not seem to notice, as if this was normal for them, it was not for us I can assure you. So, I decided to take my wife straight up to the labor and delivery floor, where we found a nurse and explained what was going on. They were able to stick us directly in a room and then an even more painful process began. We sat there in that room for hours, perhaps 3 hours. Where nurses and different doctors were constantly coming in checking on my wife, trying to find the heartbeat of both of our children. All while They fought for what felt like an eternity with the belly monitors, my wife was in visible pain and discomfort at this point. Until finally they called it an, decided that an emergency C-section had to be performed. We were devastated but had no choice but to go through with the process. The hospital had to call in a specialist from the next city over that could perform the operation. After a few hours, my son was born at 3 pounds 8 oz. He had to be rushed off to another hospital on a NICU bus, a Newborn Infant Care Unit, on a bus. Which is just one of the amazing pieces of technology that saved my son. My wife was rushed to Vanderbilt Hospital in Nashville right behind him. I decided to stay behind after discussing with my mother-in-law what had happened, she was to meet my wife at Vanderbilt so that she would not be alone. I did not want to leave my daughter, my sons twin that we lost, behind in a hospital by herself. It did not feel right to just leave her, so I stayed by myself in one of their storage closets where they kept her body until a representative from the funeral home arrived. It took quite a while; I was there for another hour or two in that room with her. There was only one nurse that checked in on me throughout the entirety of this situation unfolding, our charge nurse-who is a saint, and to this day I cannot remember her name. Only that she made a box for my wife, with pictures, and little handmade mementos from different people that have been through similar tragedies. When she was finally picked up to be taken to the funeral home for cremation, I then headed to Vanderbilt to meet up with my mother-in-law and wife, and my mother and sister who were on their way to meet us from Florida. When I arrived at the hospital, you cannot imagine my anger to learn that my mother-in-law, her own mother, had in fact not been to the hospital to be there with my wife and son. I will not go into detail about what was more important, as it still angers me to this day, that my mother from Florida drove faster than a person who lived less than 20 minutes away. My son had to spend 29 days in the NICU, under constant supervision to ensure that he would grow and be healthy. Thankfully, he is a fighter and made it through alive and well, doubling his weight within the first month and being able to be discharged from the hospital and taken home with us. It truly felt like I left a piece of my soul in that room with my daughter at the hospital, it is the most peculiar feeling. But since that day, my emotions have not worked the same, it's so much harder to cry and laugh than it used to be. Being very familiar with death and loss, I understand that this feeling will pass with time. I hope, I truly hope that this time it does not stick forever, and that I will be able to overcome this devastating loss. To add on to the anger, shortly after losing our daughter. My wife and I reached out to her ex, inquiring again about 50-50 split custody while my wife and I were grieving. To which they were adamantly against, making up whatever excuse you can imagine. Completely ignoring the fact that we just lost a child, and how much that would mean for us, and my wife especially to have her daughter with her during that time. She was not allowed to be there with my wife and son at the hospital either. Due to whatever reason that her ex has or says, it doesn't matter now as it is in the past, but it had a huge effect on us at the time. Devastatingly enough it is incredibly hard to get the court to overturn who is primary custodial parents, unless there are obvious signs of abuse and neglect. Neither here nor there but does play a role in my story.

Child Custody

Child custody is a very touchy subject, no matter who it is or what culture, poor, rich, middle class. It makes no difference which side of the aisle you are sitting on or if you even have a seat. Parenting is a difficult thing to discuss, as who is right or wrong in any parenting situation? There are a million different things that can go into each and every situation or question that pertains to it. Just because one person has a certain opinion or perspective about a certain topic within parenting, does not mean that another will share the same beliefs. My wife's custody case particularly, I feel deserves more light to the public. She was a victim of domestic violence, who did not want to ruin her husband's life or make it so that he could not see her daughter. So, she never pressed charges, and then must deal with him taking advantage of that. Pretending it never happened and that she lied about it all, passing her off as a crazy person or someone who made it all up. And it works, people believe it because there are people that lie about domestic violence all the time. So why should anyone believe that she isn't that person when they don't know her. And why would her ex say those things if they weren't true. Well, that is the real question I would say, and I would say that I think he is still in love with her. Hating the fact that she never came back, and he lost control of her. So, his only way of taking that anger out on her is to try to hurt her, the only way he can hurt her is to do everything he can to keep her from her daughter. Making up anything he chooses to. Her only way of proving it is to make enough money to take him to court and pray that her story can be portrayed in the right way. It's not hard to see it when you are involved, even as a third party if you take enough time to assess the entirety of the situation. He simply wants to maintain some semblance of control over my wife and their daughter. Which is downright not okay or should ever be allowed. And it's a hard thing to prove in a short amount of time without sounding like gossip or bickering. The way that he has treated the entire parenting relationship is that I do what I want, and you must do whatever I say because I'm the one with the power. See he has primary custodial custody due to false pretense that he presented the courts, (my wife being an alcoholic), due to not having a very good lawyer, this was allowed to be presented and I believe had a direct effect on my wife's ability to get more time with her daughter initially. That combined with the fact that she signed a piece of paper allowing him 72 to have custody in the first place, set him up to be able to have absolute control. Her ex had an impressionable hold until she worked up the courage to stand up to him and refuse to believe that he actually wants to work together with her. He has only been leading her on the entire time, hoping that she will just give up the fight. Perhaps he doesn't see it that way, perhaps he does. But regardless it is abuse, and we have both decided that it must stop, whether that mean we have to wait for my wife's daughter to be at an age where she can decide for herself or not, remains to be seen. But if that is what it comes down to, we both agreed that it would be for the best because an ugly court battle is just not going to be healthy for her. Regardless of who wins, there will be resentment that will fester for years. Which we both believe will not be healthy for her or us, or anyone involved for that matter. The manner in which he has already treated us is foul, causing untold damage in our lives as well as the lives of our children.

Manipulation

Manipulation can have profound effects on and to the mind of the person being manipulated. Especially if it goes unnoticed or suppressed for an extended period. I have seen first-hand the effects of what it did to my wife. Years of torment and being treated as though she was not to be trusted, formed her mind to feel like no one trusts her. Or even that everyone views her in the way that her ex made her view herself. That she was a liar, and was making things up, creating a situation where no one would believe her, and she was stuck. When you can't run away, and you can't speak up, it can cause very powerful things to happen in your mind. Thankfully, my wife being an incredibly strong and intelligent woman, worked up the courage to leave him early on before it did too much damage to her. However, she has not yet been able to free her daughter from what she knows will be a very unpleasant upbringing for a woman. What will be said to her daughter when she begins to explore her sexuality. Will she be labeled in a certain way by her father for wanting to be able to have relationships at the same time as growing up? Will her mother ever be able to have input in any of the important matters pertaining to her daughter, such as those relationships? Most likely not, because my wife was manipulated in the same way that her daughter is being manipulated. You see, my wife's mother split up with her father when my wife was two. And then my wife was manipulated by her mother into believing that her father was a terrible person. Who wanted to take Keiarra away from her mother forever. A very evil thing to do to a two-year-olds emotions simply out of spite, and she will begin to blame herself for all of the turmoil between her mother and father, even though none of it is her fault.

More

Growing up we lived in a trailer for quite a few years. I think we lived there up until I was in around middle school. It wasn't a bad life; the trailers were actually way nicer inside than you may think they look from the outside. I don't mind the way they look on both the outside and inside, maybe because it is what I grew up in, I'm not sure. But I do know they are cozy. We had about an acre of land, with a whole bunch of swamps behind us and forest around us. We were constantly outside; I mean this was the early nineties before the internet was really a thing like it is today. So there wasn't much to do inside besides read or eat, hangout and talk. There was TV but we didn't watch that until around time for dinner. I did love to read as a youth, but when we lived at this trailer, I was too young to read. I remember my brothers always having their friends over that played football with them. Some of them growing up to become professional athletes, it's a cool memory that I have of living in a trailer. That may be why the idea of it doesn't bother me as much as it does some. It's not about the size of the home, or where it's at, but the people that are around you and with you that really matters. Not many years later we moved to another trailer in Florida, still the same concept, just this time instead of having a swamp behind us it was orange groves and a sand mine. With rows of pine trees on either side that were farmed occasionally. We used to play all kinds of crazy games growing up. My brothers would break out their dirt bikes, and my dad and sisters on the four wheelers, kicking soccer balls around the front yard like mad men. It was crazy, and fun, and everyone loved it. I remember the neighbors thought we were all out of our minds. But we loved it, and we were free. We would go roller skating, and on field trips to learn about the country, not only the country but about the past, where we all came from and what that is supposed to mean as a people. It was a great time in the 90s. Then 9/11 happened and the internet became an early stage of what we know today, and it feels like everything started to change then. I remember it was weeks, months of constant news coverage in school and at home of what was going on in the world. Around that time, we moved into the city, because my grandparents passed away, they left a house that was right next to the high school to us. Which was perfect for us at the time since I was starting middle school, my brothers finishing high school, and my sister about to start high school. I remember when the Xbox first came out in 2002. It was awesome, my whole family sat around for days playing it that Christmas. We had rock band, and were all playing it together, jamming out as a family, laughing at my cousin trying to sing along. Amidst all the violence that was going on in the world at the time, we had some semblance of a regular world. Video games in the early 2000s really saved a lot more people than anyone gives them credit. At this house we got to experience our first bad hurricane. Hurricane Charlie came through and really tore apart everything, there were tornados on every street around us, but for whatever reason that year we didn't have any wreckage. Thankfully too, because my family put hundreds of hours of work into that house together. I learned how to work on all kinds of things thanks to my dad allowing us to be a part of that instead of hiring people to do it. I can't tell you now how much we may have disliked it at the time. There were parts that we enjoyed but manual labor is scarcely fun. Especially construction of a house, laying floor, ripping floor up, installing cabinets, drywall, tile in the bathrooms, tile in the kitchen, taking out entire walls and re doing them, there was no limit to the 80 extent of the stuff that we did to that house. It was also a tragic house, because we lived there from around 2001-2002 up until my dad passed away in 2007. I was fourteen years old, barely five feet, and weighed about two hundred pounds. Sometimes selfishly I wish he could have lived a few more years to see me lose all my weight and get into good shape, have a girlfriend and be proud of myself again. But then, who knows honestly. Sometimes I hate that I feel like the only reason I did it all was because he passed away. In my own self-hate I wanted to prove to him that I wasn't a fat, video game nerd. So, I did. But he wasn't there to see it, and that tore me apart, along with what my high school girlfriend did to me, my mind, to say the least, was in a very bad place. In high school, I did not do well, secluding myself from everyone even the teachers. I started to fail school, in eleventh grade I had lower than a 2.0 gpa and they told me that I wouldn't graduate if I didn't get it higher. So, I had to really buckle down, between eleventh and twelfth grade I retook over ten classes that I had failed for a program called grade forgiveness. Thankfully I was able to turn around my GPA and graduate with a 3.2 in the end. Needless to say, I was not going to be receiving any scholarships for my academics while I was in high school. I got my first job when I was 81 17 in a bar called Blue Martini. It was a fancy place, where I was stuck for several years. I started off in the kitchen, as a line cook, and I did that for a few years before moving out on to the floor. While working there I developed bad habits of drugs and alcohol, and it was when I turned 23 that I decided I needed to do something more with my life. Joining the military to remove myself from my bad habits, feeling that it was a combination of things keeping me in a rut. It was one of the best decisions I ever made. And took me on a new journey that, while it ultimately led to me meeting my other self. I don't regret any of it, I was able to meet my wife, who has been an amazing light in my life, and we had our children, who are also a light in my life. They are one of the few reasons that I continue to fight in this life. Working towards my dreams for them, as my dreams for me don't much matter to me anymore. I simply want them to grow up in a world that doesn't beat them down in the way that it has me. Or if it does at least, I have hopefully instilled with them a good enough foundation to help them through it. It is one of my only goals in life now is to make sure that my wife and children are set for life. Never having to worry about money and how they are going to eat the next day. It is not a pleasant experience in the modern world, as there is no way to eat or have anything in life if you are unable to work. With everything that happened to me throughout my life, I have never been able to not work until around thirty years old. And it's not that I am unable to work, but whatever happened in my mind makes it incredibly hard to be around people. It feels as though everyone is looking at me and expects the world out of me. I don't know how to explain that, but prior to my mental breakdown I never cared what other people thought of me. I was just getting through life, and now all of a sudden I am the most self conscious person you have ever met. I always was self conscious about my appearance, being fat etc. But about my status in life? No, that never bothered me before my mental breakdown, and everything that my wife's ex has said to us about not having built anything for ourselves. Or that we don't do what's best for our children, are going no where in life etc. When someone says those things to you on a constant basis, it makes you start to believe them.

www.ingramcontent.com/pod-product-compliance
Lightning Source LLC
Chambersburg PA
CBHW032118280326
41933CB00009B/892